OMNI-(Totality)

Poems and lyrics by C.L. Williams

OMNI- (Initial Phase) was written and arranged by C.L. Williams

OMNI- (Initial Phase) was edited by Jon Keesee and Luke Wood

"Rise Above" originally appeared in the anthology *Rise Above*

"Closest to Closure" originally appeared in the anthology *So Many Unsaid Things*

OMNI- (Secondary Phase) was written and arranged by C.L. Williams

OMNI- (Secondary Phase) was edited by Luke Wood

"Looking Back" originally appeared in the anthology *Reflections*

Table of Contents

<u>*OMNI- (Secondary Phase)*</u>

1. Forward
2. More than Art
3. Looking Back (Reflections Version)
4. Rent Free
5. Final Nail
6. Can't Give it Away
7. No Heroes
8. Forgotten One
9. Vilify
10. I'll Never Learn
11. Mechanical Heart
12. Hatred
13. Half the Story
14. Kiss me Goodbye
15. The Secret
16. She's Not You
17. Stitches on my Heart
18. Could've Been Me
19. Step Up
20. Fast Lane
21. Spotlight
22. Did I Lose?
23. Looking Back (Original Version)
24. Cycles
25. All on the Table

OMNI-
(Initial Phase)

OMNI- (Initial Phase)

1. Annihilate the Nihilist
2. Rise Above
3. Let My Actions Speak
4. Why Now?
5. Reminder
6. This is my Night
7. Meant for Me
8. Stop while you're Ahead
9. Go Ahead
10. Canceled
11. Watch me Fall
12. Blinded
13. Not Angry Anymore
14. Take the Pain
15. In my Head
16. As I Await
17. 37-B
18. Something to Prove
19. No Obligation
20. Luke vs C.L.
21. Hurt/Heal
22. Fake Happy Face
23. Breaking Point
24. Closest to Closure
25. Your Eulogy

Annihilate the Nihilist

Lead the world, lead them with guidance
Speaking to the world by speaking with my silence
Lead them to the new world, lead to the horizon
Show the world our love, show them our alliance
Then we will kill them all with kindness
Still go to war but we break from all the violence
And that's the way you win, annihilate the nihilist

Rise Above

I will stand because I am not afraid
I am willing to go against the grain
The words you say, they do not hurt me
Because when against hate, I will succeed
I will stand and help the defenseless
Because the gift of friendship is endless
I will not give in to hate today
Because I know it's best to walk away
I will stand against hate with the gift of love
Because when against hate, I will rise above

Let my Actions Speak

I know exactly where I stand
And I know I deserve a second chance
What's it going to be?
I think it's time I let my actions speak
I know I've messed up in the past
But mistakes should not always last
I do not want you to walk
Take a chance, let my actions talk
I know if you leave, fault is mine
But I ask that you allow me some time
Time to say why we are meant to be
As I stand here and let my actions speak

I ask once more, what will it be?
Will you allow me to let my actions speak?

Why Now?

Every moment, every milestone, you were absent
When I asked for your approval, you looked away
That point forward, I was in a self-contained exile
While you chose to forget my name
Now a spotlight shines upon me, what do I see?
Your attempt at a grand entrance back into my life
I want you to know your absence was noticed
Your silence screamed
This acceptance you show, it's rather bizarre
I know I should be thankful
But the questions are racing through my head
I'll keep it simple and ask only one
Why now?

Reminder

Every few months, I give you the same reminder
Yet you wonder why I've become an outsider
Moments like this, I feel it best to love from afar
Because the constant reminder breaks my heart
You open me up and pour salt on the wound
Not being around feels like the only thing I can do
Because when I'm around you only talk the past
Those discussions make me feel mentally harassed
I'll say it again, only this time it'll be the last
One last reminder to place upon your stash
I'm not afraid of the past, only trying to move ahead
I'm leaving the past behind, only way to ascend

This is my Night

Here it is, my moment in the light
This is my moment, my moment to shine
Every time I think I got it; it gets taken away
Difference this time, my dues have been paid
Now let me have my moment in the sun
Let me have my moment, this is the one

Because this is my night
I've been fighting for this my entire life
I'll say it again, this is my night
Moment in the sun, this feels right

This one moment will forever belong to me
For all the times I fight, all the times I bleed
This is the moment where I get to step up
This is for everyone that always showed me love
Here it is, my moment in the sun
This is my moment, this is the one

Because this is my night
I've been fighting for this my entire life
I'll say it again, this is my night
Moment in the sun, this feels right

Here it is, my moment in the light
This is my moment, my moment to shine

Because this is my night
I've been fighting for this my entire life
I'll say it again, this is my night
Moment in the sun, this feels right

Because this is my night

Meant for Me

I'm placing my throne on top of this rock
I am taking what is mine, I refuse to stop
I was born and put the silver spoon in my own mouth
From the beginning, I knew what this was about
I know who I am, what I'm meant to be
This planet it was made to be given to me

This entire world
All of this was meant for me
My place in this world
You know it was meant to be
Stop me from conquering this world
You become my enemy
Because this entire world
All of this was meant for me

I'm meant to be atop of this globe
And the top is where I will place my throne
The top is where I will be no matter what
As I am the one you will give all your trust
Follow me now or you become my enemy
Because this planet will soon be about me

This entire world
All of this was meant for me
My place in this world
You know it was meant to be
Stop me from conquering this world
You become my enemy
Because this entire world
All of this was meant for me

I will soon be the one running this place
Everywhere you go, you'll see my face
I'll be the only one you can see
Because this world was made for me!

This entire world
All of this was meant for me
My place in this world
You know it was meant to be
Stop me from conquering this world
You become my enemy
Because this entire world
All of this was meant for me

Stop While You're Ahead

Stop while you're ahead
Listen to the words, the words that I've said
Better heed my warning or you'll wind up dead

Stop while you're in the lead
If you don't stop, you'll soon face defeat
You can never win when you go against me

Stop before you fall
You better stop now before you lose it all
You better stop now, time to make the call

Stop before you cry
It's best to stop now, before you possibly die
You cannot succeed going against I

Hear the words I've said
You don't want to be next
Stop while you're ahead

Go Ahead

I know you're the one that's been throwing shade
Go ahead, step out of the shadows and say my name
If you're in the right and you know it's no doubt
Go ahead, I dare you to put my name in your mouth
If you want to run your mouth go ahead, bite me!
If you have a problem, go ahead and fight me
If you want to go then we can go right now
This won't end until one of us sees lights out

Canceled

I am the one that made the mistake
Now you want to lay me to waste
I have confessed to the mistakes I've made
Doesn't matter, you're ready to dig my grave
I am the only one paying for this sin
Only I will have the marks upon my skin
You're ready to end me, thinking you deserve justice
My fall, you are showing persistence
You won't stop until I disappear
Thinking my destruction will leave you revered
No matter how minor, I don't deserve forgiveness
You want me gone, calling me a sickness
You want me dead and that is your closure
Until then, I guess this means I'm over

Watch Me Fall

You were the first I talked to when I wasn't alright
A mistake I'll live with for the rest of my life
I thought I was speaking to a friend in confidence
In the end, I'm vilified and must face the consequence
I told you when I didn't think I could write
About letting words bleed will cost me my life

I went to you thinking I was venting to a friend
Here I go making the same mistakes once again
I don't think and say one thing I shouldn't have said
One oft-handed remark, now I'm condemned
In hindsight, that's probably what you're hoping for
Watching me fall, with my blood on the floor

Thought you were a friend, but you showed no love
All a façade, now you're ready to say I'm done
You have my number, you could've called
We could've sat down, we could've talked
Instead you decided that you wanted to watch me fall
You're on your knees praying I lose it all

I know you prefer I have nothing to my name
My one mistake, I know you want to bring shame
I know I should return the favor upon you
I'm just ready to move on, this needs to be through
Just know I really wish you the best
I really hope you soon gain success

<u>Blinded</u>

I am the villain, a confession I've already made
Your continued attacks to me, trying to dig my grave
I don't think you can see your vision is getting blurry
Because it's me the people are now showing mercy
Hatred of me is what you see, only thing in your view
What you don't are the people slowly turning on you

You've become blinded by your hatred
All of your moves, they've become so basic
Life of potential, it's becoming wasted
You've become the villain, I hope that you can face it

Hatred is the sole emotion you choose to be guiding
Giving you tunnel vision, hatred can be blinding
Turning your back on everything that you once loved
My downfall you want and now you've succumbed
I know for me, you were only wanting the worst
Only this time, you see the roles have reversed

You've become blinded by your hatred
All of your moves, they've become so basic
Life of potential, it's becoming wasted
You've become the villain, I hope that you can face it

I hope you see that the tables have turned
I hope you can change from this, I hope you'll learn
There is good in you, I know because I can see
Even if it means you have hatred towards me

You've become blinded by your hatred
All of your moves, they've become so basic
Life of potential, it's becoming wasted
You've become the villain, I hope that you can face it

Not Angry Anymore

I said it was time to get things off my chest
To avoid taking all this hatred to my death
Years have passed and my anger has calmed
My issues with you, they are not gone
It's time to move forward, with this I'm done
It's time to focus on who I will become

Time heals all wounds, you're still not forgiven
I addressed my pain to no longer feel livid
Still remember you left me when I needed you most
I still remember the emotions you provoked
It may sound bitter but you're someone I don't miss
Because you treated me as if I did not exist

Now that we've talked, our time here is through
I just wanted to tell you I no longer hate you
People in my life are limited and you don't belong
This is just me telling you goodbye, saying "So long"
I know I said we'd fight and you'd be defeated
But I've fully addressed it, I'm now completed

Take the Pain

You can keep your happiness, leave me the pain
You get the sunlight while I'm cleansed by the rain
I'll let you grab the light and begin your ascend
While I take the pain and suffer the torment
You can have the affirmations while I face the worst
I will take the pain after all I am cursed
I'll take it because I know pain has an end
I know for certain that the sun will soon ascend
Pain is temporary, memories last a lifetime
My endurance I know it is something divine
You can keep your happiness, leave me the pain
I will see the sunrise after I am cleansed by the rain

In my Head

Let the words replay
Let the moment repeat
The moment of a lifetime
All inside my head

The tragedy
The pain
The moment of hurt
Forever alive in my head

The lyrics forever hummed
The food I can always taste
The one-time moment
Always in my head

The day you said yes
Moment we became one
That special step forward
Alive in my head

The merriment
The happiness
The moment of joy
Never forgotten in my head

As I Await

I await you
As I sit here in this serene place
Wanting you to enjoy it too
But until then
I will enjoy this beauty alone

<u>37-B</u>

I ask for help, reach out to a "Friend"
But behavior makes me question the friendship again
Try to start talking, they respond "Don't ask"
They just takes my things and throw them in the bag

When corporate calls, it's genuine, not a show
I'm surprised to hear them call me "homie" and "Bro"
They call and check in, make sure I'm ok
Call me by my name, and say have a good day

Makes no sense, friends should be the kinder of two
But corporate will call and say, "What up dude!"
Half of the time, my friend won't respond to a text
Yet corporate is always checking, seeing what's best

Once all is said and done, I know how things will be
Corporate says "hi friend" my friend says
      "What up 37-B"

Something to Prove

The moments where I win, I still lose
No matter what I always have something to prove
No celebration, only moving to the next obstacle
Pleasing everyone, proven to be impossible
I master one element, another task is at hand
Regardless of the outcome I remain damned
Everything I do, you remain unimpressed
I am fallen, left with only discontent
Here I thought that you would show some love
Here I am, still wiping off the blood
I will still stand even with each cut and bruise
No matter what I always have something to prove

No Obligation

I wanted to cry the moment you ripped my heart
Your nonchalance as you ripped each string from me
Once again a victim of my own ignorance
Thinking of you as my muse, how naïve
Your lackadaisical attitude towards my feelings
That day, a sliver of me died inside
The day you said we have no obligation

Luke vs C.L.

It feels like when I talk, ridicule is guaranteed
Because my feelings only seem to matter to me
Last time I talked my feelings, I was outright ignored
The pain I felt, it was something I had to endure
When I am upset, I'm quickly told to get over myself
I'm upset over nothing and I need to seek help

But the second I start to combine paper and pen
Is the moment I receive sympathy once again
That is the moment that others show me love
Now they want to talk, now they offer a hug
Where was this when I first extended my hand
When I spoke I was treated like I am damned

Why does it take me bleeding ink for you to notice
Because when I first speak, I'm feeling hopeless
The writer and the person, they're one in the same
Yet when I speak, I am left feeling ashamed
One day I will speak and maybe others will listen
Before I am gone and left feeling distant

Hurt/Heal

HURT
This death, it is blood on your hands
Something like this? You call yourself a man?
HEAL
I heard the news, I'm sorry you lost your blood
Bring it in, I know you can use a hug
HURT
You are the creator of your own madness
You're the reason your son turned into an addict
HEAL
I'm sorry, I know I'll never understand your pain
It'll be hard moving forward, never be the same
HURT
I see what looks like you banking off of your kid
Can you not tell you're committing the ultimate sin
HEAL
Just know I'm here in case you need to converse
I don't want to see you end up in a hearse
HURT
Instead, I should wish for something worse
Spend your remaining days walking around cursed

Fake Happy Face

In this world, you are not allowed to feel down
You have to get up quick, have a quick rebound
In these times, I can't help but feel out of place
That's why in these times I put on my fake happy face

Remember when I thought you would be there for me
Your face was one I know I never did see
Even after those times I was there for you
And everything I was helping you go through
I expressed my feelings and I was called a disgrace
So at that moment I put on my fake happy face

I was going through pain and you didn't understand
It's ok you didn't, I wasn't asking for a hand
But you chose to get mad when I was feeling down
You dragged me further into the ground
But I had to keep my demeanor in this place
I did what I had to and put on my fake happy face

Maybe one day my feelings can be expressed
Because I hate when I am feeling suppressed
But for now, showing feelings is not the right way
For those times I'll have my fake happy face

Breaking Point

Many days, I wish that I do not wake
I've had more than I know I can take
No one cares about my downfall
No hands offered as I devolve to a crawl
No one hears the pains I've voiced
I am about to hit a breaking point

I'm about to break
I'm about to break
I'm about to break
Reaching a breaking point

Here I am, stuck on the ground
Yet everyone wants to kick me while I'm down
Living in this world has become too much
Telling the truth allows people to judge
I will never have love, I only receive hate
Here I am, about to break

I'm about to break
I'm about to break
I'm about to break
I am at a breaking point

I am broken and can take no more
This is the end of my internal war
I would say this is my farewell
But you don't care that I'm off to Hell
I've had more than I can take
Here I am, I'm about to break

I'm about to break
I'm about to break
I'm about to break
This is my breaking point

Here I am, already broken

Closest to Closure

Once upon a time, I thought you were a friend
If only I could see I was ignorant back then
Way back when I could never see the signs
If only then, I could see the truth and realize
When we first met you were nice, you would laugh
A friendship I thought I could never have
It wasn't long after you started acting jaded
What was once genuine, now feels like you're faking
It wasn't soon after you began to act distant
Your once kind words were now feeling less genuine
You said that I said I hated you, not what I said
Said if you picked, me or death, you'd be dead
Fallen to tears, I remember wanting to call
I wanted to apologize, see if this was all my fault
I wanted to know the right words to say
Only want a friend, I think you want me to go away
This time, I'll give in and give you want you want
I'll leave you be, friendship is over, I am done
If I could have one final wish
I wish I knew what I did to deserve this

<u>Your Eulogy</u>

I've heard the slander brought upon my name
Now it is time that I have that changed
I've heard everything, I've heard every word
Now it is time I place your body in the dirt
For your actions against me, I'm going for you neck
This is what you deserve after all of your disrespect
Your actions against me, no mercy to be had
Now it is time I get the last laugh
I want you to know, I know my own worth
Once I'm done with you, guess I'll be in church
That is when I'll tell the Priest what I did
The response will be "My child you did not sin"
Before I take you down to the morgue
I hope you've made peace with the Almighty Lord
I'll write my confession and read it to your family
Read it at your funeral, we'll call it your eulogy

OMNI-

(Secondary Phase)

<u>*OMNI- (Secondary Phase)*</u>

1. Forward
2. More than Art
3. Looking Back (Reflections Version)
4. Rent Free
5. Final Nail
6. Can't Give it Away
7. No Heroes
8. Forgotten One
9. Vilify
10. I'll Never Learn
11. Mechanical Heart
12. Hatred
13. Half the Story
14. Kiss me Goodbye
15. The Secret
16. She's Not You
17. Stitches on my Heart
18. Could've Been Me
19. Step Up
20. Fast Lane
21. Spotlight
22. Did I Lose?
23. Looking Back (Original Version)
24. Cycles
25. All on the Table

<u>Forward</u>

Be honest, you take me for granted
I'm always there, you leave me stranded
Think because I have few, I'll keep dealing with you
This is the last time I let you exclude
You claim to care but really you're toxic
I've has enough and it's making me nauseous
I know what you're thinking; I've said this before
You've overstayed your welcome, no longer adored
I'm moving forward and you're being left behind
This is necessary, call it peace of mind
Now you know I'm no longer bluffing
It's your fault that what we once had is now nothing

More than Art

I'm the last of a dying breed
I love my art but I want to succeed
A compromise or two sometimes occur
But these occasions are never meant to hurt
What i do now has become bigger than me
The money I make helps others feed
Sometimes when I talk, wallet takes the lead
That money helps dozens, not just me
All these choices, no one is at fault
Sometimes changes are needed after all
I love what I do but it's how I eat
Without it, stress takes over and I cannot sleep
I love all of this but my art is something more
But it's still my art, deep within its core

Looking Back (Reflections Version)

I've praised Heaven and I've raised Hell
No matter what I can still accept myself
I have been through the worst and I'm still alive
I've made some bad choices; I have nothing to hide
Looking back, I know I have been a disgrace
I can still look in the mirror with a smile on my face
Looking back, I've been a sinner, I've been a saint
It's my life and it is the picture that I paint
I accept the bad as it showed who I once was
I can now walk in the light and show my love
It doesn't matter because at the end of the day
I can accept the choices that I have made
Looking back, I see mistakes and accept my growth
Because I've went through things that only I know
I may've done bad, but I can now accept who I am
I can now get on my own two feet, I can now stand
You can't see it, but I've learned to accept myself
Because I've praised Heaven and I've raised Hell

<u>Rent Free</u>

How does it feel? Knowing I'm inside your mind
How does it feel? I'm invading from the inside
Know what that means? Means I'm living rent free
It also means that you must be obsessed with me
Dealing with me? It's getting harder and harder
My space in your head, it's getting larger and larger
Me in your head? Wonder what will manifest
Your hatred towards me, it's making you oppressed

Now, it's first of the month. A good day for me
You're the one paying because I'm living rent free

Final Nail

These are my closing words to you
Everything you hate about me, mostly true
The origins of your anger, I'll admit, is justified
But today, I'm not the one getting crucified
You've been running your mouth, now it's my turn
I'm setting you on fire, time for you to burn
I make a mistake, you say I never put in the work
Never responded, people knew you were berserk
Now, how about we discuss your work ethic
It's no good, it's rubbish, downright septic
You do a weeks' worth of work, months' worth of rest
This is the reason you will never have any success
Call a spade a spade, you are nothing but lazy
You want to hate me and call my work ethic shady?
I'm doing the work, my success made you envious
You wanted me to fall, you got nefarious
Let's be honest, you hate me over a lady
You have a girl but you want this one as your baby
I have now become friends with your crush
That's what ended our friendship, ended the trust
Go ahead, try telling everyone that I am wrong
Now they're turning from you and saying so long
I was the only meant for your wrath
You took down many in your unrelenting warpath
Here it is, the final, this is the final nail
You've been buried, you have failed

Can't Give it Away

An unknown, writing word after word
Writing anything, just wanting to be heard
Put it all together, finally finished the book
But no one around would give it a look
But this day was simply put, a bad day
No one would buy, couldn't even give it away

Chose to be resilient, not ready to break down
Demons were ready to place hope underground
Maybe this time, people will give it a chance
Never know about the talent at hand
Here's to any positives coming this way
Once again, overlooked, couldn't give it away

Few have taken notice but still far to go
Progress has been made, but the climb is still slow
Chances are taken and risks are being made
No one is going down, none to be slain
This day some said they're willing to pay
Some gave money and some were even given away

All the sacrifices are starting to work
Now confidence is being reaffirmed
Feelings were hurt but lessons were learned
Everything is love now that tides have turned
This was different, a very special day
People were buying, couldn't give it away

No Heroes

I've found it best to look up to none
No more hero worship, not even for one
Never meet your heroes, they only bring you down
My heroes took my spirits, put them in the ground
I choose no heroes, no one left to admire
No more heroes to look up to, to aspire

When you were knocked down, you were never out
You had a vision and you became devout
You were a trailblazer, I found it commendable
Only to discover your other actions are condemnable
We discover you're the villain, all of your insolence
They were young and you're stealing their innocence

You were a visionary, someone I'd idolize
Only to discover you are someone others agonize
I never wish to meet you, I hope that you choke
You'll never be acknowledged, not even a footnote
You are the reason I have no heroes in this universe
You're why when I see people, I only expect the worst

You are the reason I have no heroes

You were never trying to create a name
You were always willing to go against the grain
When named, you made sure others were praised
All of your actions, they left me amazed
You said you'd never sell your soul
Now it feels like money is your only goal

Once the trendsetter, now you're riding trends
Because greed is now your only ends
You're not your former self, not even a shell
You're speaking of heaven while prepping for hell
You're why I have no heroes, I now have none
With this hero worship, I can say I am done

You are the reason I have no heroes

My only inspiration, who I was yesterday
For that person, I can make it a better way
I need that person to know things can improve
My actions today, I can be the proof
These days, I need no one, I need none else
These days, my only hero is myself

I am the reason I have no heroes

Forgotten One

I am the one always putting you first
But your actions towards me, they are the worst
Half the time, you forget I exist
To be remembered, that's my only wish
You're always quick to push me aside
And I am the last one coming to your mind
Why am I always neglected
It's left me feeling disrespected
I'm not even a choice, I'm not even picked last
I am the castaway, I am the outcast
I wish I weren't who always gets the shun
I am nothing, only the forgotten one

<u>Vilify</u>

In your world, I am nothing but the bad guy
I am the one you choose to vilify
I can be one that you turn to for hate
The one you go to only to obliterate
Everything I do is wrong and you're perfect
I'm your bad guy, I only give hate and neglect
Every word I say, to you, another dreadful insult
It leads to another argument you get to catapult
Every word I say, you become analytical
Finding every reason to be spiteful and critical
Might as well be your narcissistic egotistic antithesis
To you I am the offensive one, I am the insolence
I'll take the insults while you pretend to be sane
I'm still standing as you try and bury my name

I'll Never Learn

The parallels to these stories, quite unusual
Both different, only one thing is mutual
Common denominator to both these stories, me
And how I screwed up everything that came to be
When will I change, when will I turn
One Thing I need to know, will I ever learn

One accusation ruined my relationship
Made my girl question if I'm the one she'll be with
I tried to apologize but it was far too late
One wrong move and I sealed my fate
My girlfriend, she is now my ex
I said I'd change, I'd learn respect

After fights with my ex, I said never again
Only for the same to happen to one of my friends
An argument started, I'm only to blame
Why can't I learn, when will I change
Did I forget my past crimes? Did I delete?
Because here I am sitting on repeat

I'm not healing, only making my own tomb
Instead of healing, I'm pouring salt in the wound
I hurt my friend the same way I hurt my ex
What's my problem? Why can't I give respect?
Not fanning out the flames, only adding gasoline
Instead of calming down, I'm here making a scene

I need to stop burning all of my bridges
I need to stop making all these poor decisions
Everything going wrong, all my fault
I'm the one that made the bad call
When will I change? When will I turn?
One major question; will I ever learn?

Mechanical Heart

Being human, it feels like such a chore
Want to tell God, "I don't wanna be human anymore"
Thoughts and emotions, they weigh me down
They're the reason I'll be six feet underground
Take away my humanity, I don't want to feel
All of my emotions will be easier to conceal

Take away my humanity, make me a machine
No longer a friend, now I am a fiend
If I am mechanical, I will never be hurt
No more pain I will have to exert
Not turning my back, they've already turned on me
This is my request, this is my decree

Remaining human means my ventricles will burst
Make me mechanical so I'll never feel the worst
Make me a machine and take away my flesh
This isn't my end, this is what I call progress
This'll be the last time I'm emotionally torn apart
I'll be a machine with a mechanical heart

<u>Hatred</u>

I hate you so much I can't even breathe
Why are you in my life, why can't you leave
You are my enemy and I want you dead
Never be friends, we can never break bread
Being around you, it makes my blood boil
I see you and want your neck in a coil
You are a cancer crawling in my skin
Wanting you dead, even God can forgive this sin
As I see you my anger continues to grow
Will not stop until I see you are six feet below
You are a cancer and I will stop this infection
Next time I see you, as I look into my reflection

Half the Story

You say you know, you don't truly understand
The sadness in my life, where I currently am
You think it is a phase and that I'll be ok
If you only knew my thoughts each and every day
You say get over it, you don't feel my pain
I tell you the truth, you ignore what I'm saying
You know half the story, other half you ignore
You walk away, say you don't want to hear anymore
Bet you didn't know I cried myself to sleep that night
I even contemplated taking my own life
You never even asked if I was alright
I have nothing, I have no one by my side
Just know if I'm not alright, if this is the end
Your last words to me were "Just get over it"
You know only half the story, only one side
You only know pieces and fractions of my life

<u>Kiss me Goodbye</u>

Talking to my love over the phone
Haven't seen you recently, I'm feeling alone
For now, phone chatter must suffice
Must admit, hearing your voice, it's quite nice
But our conversation time is nigh
You tell me through the phone "kiss me goodbye"

Placing my hand upon your beautiful face
Seeing you here, speaking your name
Love in the air as you hear my breathing in your ear
Holding you close, holding you near
Only this night was ours, no one kissing goodbye
You turned towards me and said "kiss me goodnight"

Growing pains of love can cause great strains
Now we only give arguments and complaints
Packed your bags and said you needed your space
Last time I thought I would see your face
This time I knew things had went awry
When you left, you didn't even kiss me goodbye

I knew it was over, it was time to let go
Can I move on? I don't think even God will know
How can someone I once loved have no meaning
It was once love, now it's only fighting and screaming
I showed no emotion, I swallowed my pride
I just left this time I chose to wave goodbye

The Secret

The feelings I have for you, I know that it's love
If I were to tell the truth, you might not say no
Why turn down love? How can I be so ignorant?
Why would I put myself through such detriment?
I know we're compatible, we could be together
The truth is I love you but I know you deserve better
The dilemma we have is mine and it's mine alone
To better tell you, I'll let the dilemma be known

It's said the best thing to give your lover is your time
I can't give you a thing I have problems calling mine
It's also said to give your lover your very heart
How can I give you something that's fallen apart?
Can't have you come in my life, expect you to repair
That's not doing right by you, that is unfair
If I'm getting the best of you, you deserve the same
If I couldn't do that, that would be a shame

Best thing for my feelings, best to let them hide
You won't hurt if I let my secret eat me alive
Keeping this a secret means you'll never be hurt
You'll find someone who'll give you more worth
I'm doing this for you, I'm doing what's best
You deserve a whole heart, not just what's left
My secret being told, maybe that time will come
Until then, this is my secret and I share with none

She's Not You

She is willing to give me her heart
She wants to have a family with me
She's told me countless times she loves me
I know she tells me the truth
I know a future with her could be grand
I know she would put me before her
My heart cannot love her the same
My heart cannot let go of another
My heart belongs to someone else
The truth is, "Loving her" will hurt us both
The truth is, she doesn't have my heart
The truth is, she's not you

<u>Stitches on my Heart</u>

Every battered bit, every shattered piece
Can you accept the broken aspects of me
I am someone still learning how to heal
Will you accept that I am trying to rebuild
I ask of your acceptance, please do not run
Is my brokenness something you can confront
Will you be close or will you love me from afar
Can you accept that I have stitches on my heart

Will you put stitches on my heart
Is my love something you'll embark
Please know I'm learning to love again
Can my love be something you extend

I know our feelings for one another are the same
Can you love someone that is emotionally drained
My heart says you can love me for who I am
Is me in your future something you have planned
Just know if you are broken I'll help heal you too
Can I be there for everything that you'll go through
Will you be close or will you love me from afar
Can you accept that I have stitches on my heart

Will you put stitches on my heart
Is my love something you'll embark
Please know I'm learning to love again
Can my love be something you extend

Could've Been Me

I saw you in passing the other day
Hard to believe things could've went another way
I know it's difficult for many to believe
But at one point, it could've been you and me
Once upon a time it was you and I in bed
Thinking we were in love, this would never end
Saying we'd have something we'd call our own
We'd be together, be each other's home
It could've been me standing next to you
I'd see you walk down the aisle, we'd say "I do"
But this was a future that never did happen
I take full responsibility for all of my actions
I should've told you that I wasn't ready
Heat of the moment, things just got heavy
You were my first, wasn't meant to last
We both knew this time would eventually pass
We've moved on, best for both of us
Even through the drama and the fuss
There is one thing I occasionally think of, only one
It could've been me, father of your son

Step Up

My opinion is now a method of persuasion
I'm now having to live up to expectations
What I do now, isn't just me, it goes beyond
What I say, what I do, many have become quite fond
Time I step up, reach that next level
Doing this for other now, can't just settle
I'm now in a leader role, they choose to follow
Need to be transparent, no longer acting hollow
Everything now, it's treated as a status
Now is the time to let go of all malice
So I'll step it up now, give you more of me
As we reach the next level of our destiny

Fast Lane

With all of these changes, life is moving so fast
Itchy finger on the trigger, got my foot on the gas
Do I drive off in the sunset or cock, aim, and shoot
Praise my decision now, later on that decision is moot
Am I making the right decision or am I just going mad
Am I ready for the life I thought I could never have
This is the fast lane, there is no time to think twice
But if that decision is wrong, that decision is my life
Maybe I should go trigger happy, only care for myself
Even though others led me to this new life of wealth
Maybe I'll keep driving and shoot anyone in my way
That's how it goes when it is life in the fast lane

Spotlight

Now I'm putting the spotlight on me
Making money off a product I was giving for free
Now you want to hate, calling me fake
That's because I'm the one taking checks to the bank
I'm now the one moving up in the rankings
Now my success is your own rude awakening
The truth is I am everything you are not
Last time I checked, I'm the one at the top
The truth is you're lazy and you can't get by
What was once my side hustle has me in the high life
I know you want to hate but look at me now
Haven't even made it I'm the one they go to for clout

Did I Lose?

Sharing my work with the world
Drawing the unknown to me
Waiting to see what unfolds
Be it good or be it bad
And now I ask, can I lose?

It's friendly competition
But I'm on the losing end
Don't go down without a fight
Though I accept my defeat
And now I ask, did I lose?

A battle lost, a war won
My work is drawing them in
Now the victor, yet I won
It may not make sense to you
I ask again, did I lose?

Primary goal, a success
My work shared, followers gained
They're ready for my next move
Loss to you, victory mine
Say it again, did I lose?

Looking Back (Original Version)

I've praised Heaven and I've raised Hell
No matter what I can still accept myself
I have been through the worst and I'm still alive
I've made some bad choices; I have nothing to hide
Looking back, I know I have been a disgrace
I can still look in the mirror with a smile on my face

Looking back, I've been a sinner and I've been a saint
It's my life and it is the picture that I paint
I accept the bad as it showed who I once was
I can now walk in the light and show my love
It doesn't matter because at the end of the day
I can accept the choices that I have made

Looking back, I see my mistakes, accept my growth
Because I've went through things that only I know
I may have done bad, but I can now accept who I am
I can now get on my own two feet, I can now stand
You may not see it but I've learned to accept myself
Because I've praised Heaven and I've raised Hell

Cycles

It's not always sun, the moon will soon rise
Just like it doesn't always rain, we will get sunshine
It's not always dark, the light will get its turn
But it's also not always rainbows, we sometimes hurt
This is life and life has its cycles

Not all is fun, the party eventually ends
But not everything is work, vacation soon begins
Sometimes you're front and center, others the back
Eventually you'll be where you want to be at
This is life and life has its cycles

Everything in life always comes back around
Before then, we take turns, go upside down
We even get taken for a tailspin
As the saying goes, the end is where we begin
This is life and life has its cycles

All on the Table

I've confessed to being the villain
I have admit to falling in love
I've shown my feelings towards the past
I've talked all my dream scenarios
I have placed my heart upon my sleeve
I've admit loved ones have walked away from me
I said closure is one thing I'll never have
I've confessed all of my secrets
I spoke of my darkest thoughts
I talk about the ongoing war within myself
I have left it all on the table
I've shed all to show I am UNBREAKABLE

Five Seven Five Preview

The next book from C.L. Williams is titled *Five Seven Five* and is a haiku collection. Here are eight haiku that will be featured in the upcoming collection.

Who am I to you?

Who am I to you?
Am I the one that you love
Or only a friend

Stop Hate with Love

Let's stop hate with love
Be kind to one another
Show others your heart

Embrace Change

Embrace the changes
Never know what it will bring
Greet with open arms

Escape?

Are we near the end?
Can you see the light ahead?
Ready to escape?

The Coming Storm

There's a storm coming
You need to be more prepared
Its time is nearing

Another Day

A beautiful day
The trees swaying in the wind
The bees buzz around

<u>Songbird</u>

Beautiful Songbird
Playing its melodic song
A new song begins

<u>The Wake</u>

Today is the Wake
The time to get full closure
Say final goodbyes

Coming soon!

Five Seven Five (Haiku Collection)

Collapsing Worlds (Science Fiction short story collection)

With All of my Heart (Romance short story collection)

Unbreakable (Poetry book)

Books available by C.L. Williams

Poetry Books
Awakening with the Sea (written as Luke Wood)
Lies of the Fearless (written as Luke Wood)
Aspects of Love (written as Luke Wood)
Approaching Humanity (written as Luke Wood)
META- (Complete) (written as Luke Wood)
The Paradox Complex
OMNI- (Totality)
Elsewhere
Five Seven Five
Unbreakable (Coming Soon)

Fiction Books
Veering Straight Ahead (written as Luke Wood)
Wretched Scars (cowritten with Ray Labuen)
Three Crowns
The Escape of Ernest Frost
Dream Awake
The Next Step
The Next Step: First Valentine's
Lucifer's Lost Love
Playing Games
Cindy's Choice
Demonic Bites
Sector Omicron
Tales from the Forbidden Forest
Regroup from the Remains
Collapsing Worlds (Coming Soon)
With All of My Heart (Coming Soon)

Anthologies featuring C.L. Williams

Mystery Monster 13
Sideshow
Evil Lurks
After: Undead Wars
Flash Fiction Addiction
WORLDS: Dark Drabbles #1
ANGELS: Dark Drabbles #2
MONSTERS: Dark Drabbles #3
Storming Area 51
Poetica
BEYOND: Dark Drabbles #4
UNRAVEL: Dark Drabbles #5
Eerie Christmas
APOCALYPSE: Dark Drabbles #6
Scary Snippets: Christmas
Dark Moments: Year One
Portal: Inner Circle Writers' Group
Malediction
One of Us
Who's Who of Emerging Writers 2020
ANCIENTS: Dark Drabbles #10
Beyond the Grave
Midnight Writers
As I Learnt to Fly
Until then, There's Coffee
Poetica 2
So Many Unsaid Things
Cooch Behar Anthology

ABOUT THE AUTHOR C.L. Williams is an international bestselling author currently living in central Virginia. He released seven poetry books and one cowritten book under his real name; Luke Wood. In 2017, Three Crowns was his first release under the name C.L. Williams.

2018 saw the release of five books in a single calendar year; The Paradox Complex, The Escape of Ernest Frost, Dream Awake, Aspects of Love 1.5, and The Next Step. 2018 also saw C.L. Williams have his first visual adaptation, "Sad Crying Clown" from The Paradox Complex was turned into a short film by Matthew Mark Hunter of MMH Productions. 2018 also saw his poem "Homecoming" become an award-winning poem.

In 2019, C.L. Williams put his efforts into anthology releases, ending the year with a total of 52 publications. C.L. Williams managed bestselling status in 2019 and was a part of multiple releases peaking at number one in various genres.

In 2020, C.L. Williams announced his novelette collection, Chaos Fusion. With the first release Lucifer's Lost Love becoming a best seller, the first release with C.L. Williams as the sole author to become a best seller. His follow-up, Cindy's Choice, became his first number one as a sole author. He also released his fifth novella *Tales from the Forbidden Forest*.

In 2021, C.L. Williams released the first half of his poetry book *OMNI-* titled *OMNI- (Initial Phase)* while continuing to appear in anthologies and attending conventions and festivals. In 2022, C.L. Williams released the second half of *OMNI-* titled *OMNI- (Secondary Phase)* along with its physical release, *OMNI- (Totality)*. He also released his first haiku collection, *Five Seven Five*.

Keep Updated

Facebook
www.facebook.com/writer434

Twitter
@writer_434

Instagram
@writer434

YouTube
YouTube.com/c/writer434

YouTube (Second Channel)
YouTube.com/c/CLWilliamsOfficial

Blog
Writer434.wordpress.com

Thank you for reading!